T E X   M

MW01093320

Traditions
— A N D —
Spirit

BY C. J. BIBLE
ILLUSTRATIONS BY
MARSHALL PETERSON

Texas A&M: Traditions and Spirit

ISBN: 0-9627306-0-2

Printed in Texas, USA

Dedication

To D. X. Bible and his brother Hollis U. Bible,
for their love of Texas A & M University.

CONTENTS

ILLUSTRATIONS

FOREWORD

I need to admit something right up front. I'm not an Aggie. On the contrary, I went to "t.u.," as Aggies call The University of Texas. And that's not all. My husband Jon is a "teasip," as are some of my family and friends. I worked at UT for over 15 years. And I have a lot of pride in my school.

Why is a UT grad writing about A&M traditions? Like so many others, I've long been fascinated with Aggies. As a student caught up in the keen A&M-UT rivalry, I heard bits and pieces about the "spirit of Aggieland" that made me curious and even a bit jealous. What made Aggies so dedicated to the school? After graduating, I married a man whose father (Hollis U. Bible) had attended and played football at A&M, whose uncle (D. X. Bible) coached football there, whose godfather (John C. Mayfield) is in the Hall of Honor, and whose longtime family friend (Tommy Mills) is in the Athletic Hall of Fame. Besides impressing me with their warmth and openness, they and other Aggies I have met instilled in me a sense of the uniqueness of the school, its spirit and traditions. And the fact that A&M now has over 40,000 students has not made Aggies any less friendly or aware of their heritage.

The impetus to actually write this book came from my niece Sherri, a high school student interested in attending A&M despite her father's staunch "UT or else" attitude. She made me see how much the Aggie spirit affects even the young — bucking a father with orange and white in his veins is, after all, not a task for the fainthearted — and made me eager to know what produces that spirit and makes Aggies such diehards all their lives.

And the project left me with even more respect for the "institution" — a word applicable in more ways than one — of A&M than I began with. At a time when college campuses have become larger and so complicated and students are offered many distractions, A&M manages to maintain its caring and supportive climate. It provides former students with an anchor for their lives and current ones with a nurturing educational environment. I believe its spirit and traditions hold up more strongly as the years go by.

I owe some people thanks for their help with this book. My friend Tim Henderson (Class of '80) reviewed the draft and offered suggestions resulting from his "on the job" training as a student. Major Jake Betty (Class of '73), Cadet Training Officer, spent much time verifying my "facts" and providing details based on his long affiliation with the school. My husband Jon donated his support and editing skills. Finally, thanks to the Aggies whose indomitable spirit so intrigued me in the first place.

c.b.

INTRODUCTION

Texas A&M University is known throughout the country for its unique spirit and traditions, most of which originated in the Corps of Cadets. Although fewer students are in the Corps today, in the beginning all students — early on, A&M admitted only males — were cadets. While students at other colleges flocked to fraternities and social clubs, the Corps was the only fraternity for Aggies. This encouraged the student body to develop as a cohesive, supportive group.

These traditions are explored in the following pages. For easy reading, an effort has been made to "hit the highlights" — to discuss, in other words, the traditions that are the most prominent and the major source of the "spirit of Aggieland." Some Aggies, of course, may have different versions of the traditions discussed in this book. They may think that something should have been included that wasn't, or that something included didn't happen quite that way. Despite the possibility of differing opinions, one can be sure that all Aggies believe strongly in their traditions and hold them close to their hearts.

PART 1

THE CAMPUS

TEXAS A&M -- A QUICK HISTORY

The first public institution of higher education in this state, the Agricultural and Mechanical College of Texas was established on April 17, 1871. On that date, the Twelfth Texas Legislature appropriated $75,000 to this land grant college for the construction of academic buildings and accommodations for professors. On June 21, commissioners appointed by Governor Edmond Davis acquired title to three tracts of land in Brazos County. In the first of these transactions, a Mr. Harvey Mitchell transferred 980 acres to A&M.

A&M formally opened its doors to students on October 2, 1876. The Texas Constitution of 1876 declared the new college "a branch of The University of Texas, for instruction in agriculture, the mechanic arts and the natural sciences connected therewith." Considered part of a university not yet in existence — The University of Texas at Austin opened in 1883 — A&M was governed by a Board of Directors which had exclusive authority over the college. With 5,200 acres, A&M had at that time the largest campus of any institution in the country.

During its early years, A&M taught only classical subjects, as its faculty was experienced only in these areas. Few thought then that "farming" could be taught to anyone, and indeed many students attended A&M to get away from farming. In 1880, A&M expanded its curriculum to include training in both agricultural and mechanical subjects. Before 1885, students who completed an established subject curriculum received certificates; in that year, Walter Wipprecht was awarded the first diploma.

For many years, funding for A&M was a perplexing problem and a source of contention between the school and UT. Finally, in 1930, the University of Texas Regents and the Directors of A&M agreed that A&M would receive a third of the University endowment. This endowment, called the Available Fund, consists of the proceeds from the investment of revenue from the Permanent Fund, which in turn consists of revenue from land and oil leases in West Texas. In 1931, the Legislature allotted one third of the Available University Fund to A&M and two-thirds to the University of Texas.

In 1963, the Legislature changed the school's name from the Agricultural and Mechanical College of Texas to Texas A&M University. Not everyone was pleased with this, however — indeed, many Aggies thought the change took the heart out of A&M and deprived it of its special identity. Many still insisted on calling the university "A.M.C.," and some do so today, including singing A. M. C. in the lyrics of the school song, "The Spirit of Aggieland."

A&M grew rapidly, becoming a university of national prominence with over 40,000 students and degree programs offered in eleven separate colleges. The current branches of the Texas A&M University System are:

Texas A&M University
Texas A&M International University
Texas A&M University-Commerce
Texas A&M University-Corpus Christi
Texas A&M University-Kingsville
Texas A&M University-Texarkana
Prairie View A&M University
Tarleton State University
West Texas A&M University
Baylor College of Dentistry
Texas Transportation Institute

Texas Animal Damage Control Service
Texas Veterinary Medical Diagnostic Laboratory
Texas Forest Service
Agricultural Extension Service
Agricultural Experiment Station
Engineering Extension Service
Engineering Experiment Station

At first, A&M accepted only men. Women, however, soon began participating in college life, although not as official students. In 1893, for example, Ethel Hutson, the daughter of a professor, began attending classes, though she received no credit. Her twin sisters, Sophie and Mary, completed the requirements for a civil engineering degree in 1903, but they received "certificates of completion" rather than degrees. Other women attended summer classes, prompting the Board of Directors in 1915 to make its first official policy statement excluding women from regular sessions. However, women — primarily relatives of employees and members of local families — continued to attend the school unofficially, with the knowledge and tacit approval of administrators.

In the 1930's, a court order to force A&M to officially admit women was unsuccessfully sought. The status quo continued until the 1960's, when the Board of Directors agreed to admit women on a limited basis beginning on June 1, 1963. By the fall of 1969, all women who could meet the academic standards set for male applicants were admitted. In 1972, a women's dormitory was provided for the regular session. Women now comprise over 40% of the enrollment.

For more than 100 years, A&M has served the people of Texas well. Though it has changed to meet the new needs and interests of its students and the people of this state, the university has remained true to its dedication to outstanding teaching, research and service.

OLD MAIN

Old Main (pictured below), the first building on campus, was completed in 1875 at a cost of $100,000. This structure, however, along with all college records, was destroyed by fire on May 27, 1912; subsequently, a Mr. Frederick Giesecke was chosen to design a new building. The Academic Building erected on the site was completed in 1914 and is a fine example of revival architecture. It faces the Albritton Tower and a main entrance to the campus. The original light on its dome — which students repeatedly shot out in the early years — was called Prexy's Moon. A mosaic Seal of the University, donated by the Class of 1978, is on the rotunda floor.

SBISA HALL

The dining hall was named for Bernard Sbisa, an outstanding chef who ran it from 1879 to 1928, becoming an institution on campus himself. Known as the Old Mess Hall, the building burned down on November 11, 1911. That was the only day during his tenure at A&M on which Sbisa missed serving a scheduled meal — and even then he managed to serve a LATE breakfast. Construction on the new Sbisa Hall began in May, 1912. Frederick Giesecke was also the architect for this project.

ALBRITTON BELL TOWER

The Albritton Tower is 138 feet high and houses a 49-bell Carillon programmed to sound like the Westminster Chimes. The bronze bells play in four octaves and vary in weight from 28 to 6,550 lbs. Finished in 1984, the Tower was a gift of Mr. Ford Albritton (Class of '43). Twenty-four of its bells are dedicated to members of the Albritton family, friends of A&M or former University officials, and are inscribed with the person's name and, in some cases, a short phrase about the individual. Special pieces are played for University occasions such as commencement, commissioning, Silver Taps, and military reviews. Four six-foot clocks adorn each side of the Tower.

MEMORIAL STUDENT CENTER

The Memorial Student Center is one of the prominent buildings on campus. Dedicated on April 21, 1951, to the memory of A&M men who gave their lives for their country, the Center was built to foster the social, cultural and recreational phases of student life. On the dedication stone, these words appear beside the names of fallen Aggies:

> In humble reverence this building is dedicated to those men of A&M who gave their lives in defense of our country. Here is enshrined in spirit and in bronze enduring tribute to their

valor and to their deep devotion. Here their memory shall remain forever fresh — their sacrifices shall not be forgotten. Gratitude is due those thousands of former students of this college who provided the initial incentive to erect this structure and made liberal contributions to its cost. In their behalf and that of the generous people of Texas as a whole who made possible its completion, this center has been created. May it serve as a useful memorial to the heroic sons of A&M who gave their all, enriching the lives of thousands of young Texans now living and others yet unborn.

In 1974, a major expansion of the MSC was finished, and another expansion is now underway. The Center and the grass areas around it are memorial areas. The Grove is a recreational area used by the MSC for various events.

STATUE OF LAWRENCE SULLIVAN ROSS

Lawrence Sullivan ("Sul") Ross became president of A&M after completing a term as Governor of Texas and served from 1891 to 1898. His appointment gave A&M new prominence and respect and thus was a turning point in its development. Ross is considered the founder of the "Aggie tradition" due to his emphasis on the Corps of Cadets, military training, and *esprit de corps*, as well as his own personal example.

Born in 1838 in Bentonsport, Iowa, Ross and his family came to Texas a year later. Early in life Ross protected his family from the Comanche Indians, and eventually became a Texas Ranger. He was later a Confederate Army officer and a famous Indian fighter, and before becoming Governor he was a county sheriff and a state Senator. Ross ended his career by becoming the president of A&M, dying in office on January 3, 1898.

Because Ross embodied the spirit of A&M so well, a bronze statue of him (pictured right) was commissioned by legislative grant to sculpter Pompeo Coppini. Unveiled on May 4, 1919, the statue stands in front of the Academic Building. It is the focus of an Aggie tradition: In 1933, two upperclassmen found a bottle of brass polish as they were packing to go home. Rather than throw it away, they ordered several freshmen to use it to polish the statue. Students today still keep the statue brightly polished in honor of this A&M founding father.

MEMORIAL OAKS

On February 23, 1920, oak trees were planted as memorials to men who had died in World War I. The Corps gathered on the main drill field in full military dress as the Board of Directors and Dr. W. B. Bizzell, A&M president, presided over the planting of 55 trees. The trees encircled the drill field to represent the honor roll of Aggie citizen- soldiers who had died in combat, with markers at the base of each tree serving as memorials. This drill field, which has been used as the

parade ground for Corps reviews since 1876, was named in honor of General Ormond R. Simpson (Class of '36), who for years headed the School of Military Sciences. In recent years it has also been used for intramural athletics as well as for Corps reviews.

WESTGATE WAR MEMORIAL

The Westgate War Memorial was a gift of the Classes of 1923-26 designed to commemorate former students who died in World War I. It is located on the northwest corner of the Drill Field, Simpson Field. The inscription on the Memorial is as follows:

> In recognition of the splendid participation by the A&M College of Texas in the World War and of the heroic sacrifices made by her sons. This memorial is given by the classes of 1923-24-25-26.

CANNONS

In 1910, A&M received the Distinguished Institution Award from the United States War Department, designating it as one of the top ten military institutions in the nation. In addition to

naming a graduating senior as a second lieutenant in the U. S.
Army, the War Department gave A&M two breech-loading
rifled cannons with carriages and equipment from the Army.
These were prized equipment for the Corps of Cadets and were
manned by seniors who had not received appointments as cadet
officers.

YMCA

The Alumni Memorial YMCA was funded by the alumni in
1912. Frederick Giesecke, the architect for so many other A&M
buildings, designed this one as well.

WE'VE NEVER BEEN LICKED

A war movie was filmed at A&M in 1943. It involved a student
in the Corps of Cadets who is posthumously honored at Kyle
Field. The film was produced by Walter Wanger and directed by
Jack Rawlins with a script by Norman Reilly Raine; actors included Richard Quine and Noah Berry, Jr.

PART 2

THE AGGIES

THE "AGGIES"

In the early 1900's, students at A&M were referred to as "Farmers." "Aggie" began to be used as a nickname in the 1920's and was officially adopted as the student-body nickname in 1949, when the name of the school yearbook was changed from *The Longhorn* to *Aggieland.* Students have been widely referred to as "Aggies" since approximately the end of World War II.

The Aggie Code of Honor states that Aggies will not lie, cheat or steal, or tolerate those who do.

AGGIE SPIRIT

To define the "Aggie Spirit" is impossible. Aggies, however, know what it is, and all have it. Virtually anyone who meets or sees Aggies, moreover, has a good sense of what it is. But if two Aggies were asked to define that spirit, their definitions would likely differ in some respects.

Aggie Spirit is pride in the university — the education received, the campus, the athletic teams, the band, the Corps, and everything else that makes up A&M. It is the friendliness and family feeling an Aggie has for all who have attended A&M. It is the character that affects the way Aggies live the rest of their lives. It is respect for the school and what it represents, and for all fellow Aggies. Most of all, it is the traditions which have developed over the years, which have made A&M so respected and envied around the country.

AGGIE JOKES

The first Aggie joke originated around 1937. The Aggie joke became well-known in 1965 with the publication of *101 Aggie Jokes* by an Aggie, the sister of an Aggie and a graduate of TCU.

An Aggie offered this example of an Aggie joke:

Two Aggies decided to go ice fishing. They got together all of their equipment and headed out onto the ice. As they prepared to cut a hole in the ice, a booming voice cried out:
"THERE ARE NO FISH UNDER THE ICE"
The Aggies were amazed. What a loud voice! Where was it coming from? What did it mean? They continued their preparations. The voice boomed out again:
"THERE ARE NO FISH UNDER THE ICE"
The two Aggies began to get concerned. What could this be? One Aggie looked at the other Aggie and said, "That must be GOD!" The voice came again:
"NO, I'M NOT GOD. I'M THE MANAGER OF THIS ICE SKATING RINK!"

Another example:

An Aggie was going out for a night on the town with a friend. His friend met him and they started out. As they walked along, his friend looked down and noticed the letters "TGIF" on his boots.

"What does TGIF mean?" asked his friend.

"You mean, you don't know?!?" the Aggie asked incredulously. "It means, 'Toes Go In First.'"

MAROON AND WHITE

The A&M colors were red and white until 1921, when a poem was published in *The Texas Aggie* to congratulate former Aggie football coach Charlie B. ("Uncle Charlie") Moran for being chosen to the NCAA Coaches Hall of Fame. In that poem, "maroon" was used to rhyme with "soon." In 1923, the color of the football jerseys was changed to maroon. It was likely just a coincidence that the football being carried down the field by the players blended almost indistinguishably into the new color.

OFFICIAL SEAL

The official university seal was adopted in September of 1947. According to the minutes of the Board of Directors of March 28-29 of that year, the seal

> shall consist of a star of five points, imposed upon a "T" and encircled, on one side by a live oak branch, and on the other by a laurel branch. At the base of the "T" shall be the date 1876, the official opening of the College, and circling the outer rim of the seal shall be the words, "The Agricultural and Mechanical College of Texas."

AGGIE WAR HYMN

The Aggie War Hymn was written by J. V. "Pinky" Wilson, a former student, as he stood guard with the American Expeditionary Forces on the Rhine at the end of World War I. It was introduced as a school tradition in 1920 and put on paper by George Fairleigh in 1921. The War Hymn's lyrics are as follows:

> Hullabaloo, Canek! Canek!
> Hullabaloo, Canek! Canek!
> Goodbye to Texas University
> So long to the Orange and the White.

Good luck to dear old Texas Aggies,
They are the boys that show the real old fight.
The eyes of Texas are upon you,
That is the song they sing so well, sounds like hell.
So good-bye to Texas University,
We're going to beat you all to hell.
Chig-ga-raa-gar-em!
Chig-ga-raa-gar-em!
Rough! Tough!
Real Stuff! Texas A&M.

The War Hymn concludes with the chant, "Saw Varsity's horns off, Varsity's horns are sawed off." During the chant, Aggies stand united, with ankles crossed over the ankles of the next person, and their arms around each other (pictured left). Everyone moves as one, back and forth from side to side.

THE SPIRIT OF AGGIELAND

The school song was written in 1925 by an A&M junior, Marvin Mimms, and was introduced to the student body that fall. The music was composed by bandmaster Richard Dunn. Its lyrics are as follows:

Some may boast of prowess bold,
Of the school they think so grand,
But there's a spirit can ne'er be told,
It's the spirit of Aggieland.

We are the Aggies - the Aggies are we,
True to each other as Aggies can be,
We've got to FIGHT, boys,
We've got to FIGHT!
We've got to fight for maroon and white.
After they've boosted all the rest,
They will come and join the best,
For we are the Aggies-the Aggies so true.
We're from Texas A. M. U.

T-E-X-A-S, A-G-G-I-E,
Fight! Fight! Fight-fight-fight!
Fight! Maroon! White-white-white!
A-G-G-I-E, Texas! Texas! A-M-U!
Gig'em, Aggies! 1! 2! 3!
Farmers Fight! Farmers Fight!
Fight-Fight-Fight
Fight-Fight-Fight
Farmers, Farmers, Fight!

ASSOCIATION OF FORMER STUDENTS

The first meeting of an Alumni Association was held in July of
1880. The Association was officially formed in 1880 to furnish
spiritual support and funds for A&M. In 1921, its name became
the Association of Former Students. Unlike other university
graduates, Aggies are known as "former students" rather than "ex-
students." Everyone who graduates from A&M is automatically
a member of the Association of Former Students; active membership is based on yearly contributions to the Annual Fund. Active
or not, all former students receive mailings which keep them in
touch. Membership in the Association signifies that the graduate will forever be affiliated with the University — once an
Aggie, always an Aggie, in other words.

On May 27, 1918, the Class of 1898 held the first Class Reunion on campus. Official Reunions are now held every five years
by every graduating class. While most schools struggle to attract
former students for reunions every 10-20 years, Aggies successfully gather far more often. Former students observing their 50th
anniversaries are inducted into the Lawrence Sullivan Ross
Group and presented with "Golden Circle" certificates recogniz-
ing them for their devotion to and interest in A&M.

The Annual Fund of the Association of Former Students
affords unrestricted funds for the support of A&M's academic en-
deavors and the work of the Association, including student scholarships, an alumni publication, *The Texas Aggie*, the Directory of
Former Students, Faculty Teaching Awards, The Aggie Band,
and Bonfire. The Century Club, organized in 1965, has become
the backbone of the Fund. Originally, membership in this Club
required a $100 donation (Bronze membership); in 1970, other
donor categories were established, including the $250 Silver
Century membership, $500 Gold Century membership and
$1,000 Diamond Century membership. The Club now has over
20,000 members, with new member opportunities including the
$2,000 Double Diamond and the $15,000 Endowed Diamond.

The Development Foundation was chartered in 1949 by the

Association to raise large gifts for restricted projects, including endowed professorships, building construction, and student scholarships. The Foundation obtains gifts not only from former students, but also corporations, foundations and trusts. The Opportunity Awards, another Association program, gives scholarships to students who excel academically and in extracurricular activities.

In 1973, the Forsyth Alumni Center, named in honor of J. M. "Cop" Forsyth (Class of '12), was opened in the southwest wing of the Memorial Student Center. The drive to locate the Forsyth Center there, in the heart of the campus, was led by Ford Albritton (Class of '43). In 1987, with the opening of the Alumni Center at a new site, the space occupied by the Forsyth Center became an art gallery. Known as the Forsyth Gallery, it houses the Runyon Collection.

The new Alumni Center is named for Clayton Williams, Jr. (Class of '54) in honor of his contributions to the Association and his continuing support for A&M in many areas. This crescent-shaped building, the largest stand-alone alumni center in the country, was built as much as a resource for A&M as to serve the needs of the Association. Designed and built by former students, it was financed by a large gift from Clayton Williams, Jr., and gifts from other former students. The impressive center represents the dedication and support of the Former Students' Association for Texas A&M.

PART 3

THE STUDENT BODY

THE STUDENT BODY

A&M has a student body of over 40,000 students. Despite this large number, Aggies maintain the friendly campus atmosphere through the tradition of saying "Howdy" to passersby as they move around campus. Indeed, the open and enthusiastic friendliness of Aggies sets A&M apart from other universities. People visiting the campus are often surprised and delighted by the welcoming atmosphere.

This tradition began in the Corps of Cadets. Early on, freshman cadets were required to "whip out" their hands to shake with upperclassmen. They also had to tell their names, hometowns and majors, and each cadet had to remember the other's name. This tradition continues today, with all cadets learning each others' names and all Aggies speaking to strangers on campus.

FISH

A&M freshman are called "fish." This term was first used by cadets in the 1880's to refer to new students. To them, fish represented a raw, slightly odious and lowly creature swimming in waters over its head, and seemed an appropriate designation. Their backgrounds notwithstanding, all fish are regarded as inferior to upperclassmen. A fish who enters A&M at mid-term has been referred to as a "frog," and students who enter after the freshman year have been said to have "frogged in."

Fish Camp is an orientation for Freshmen held before school begins in the fall. Established in 1954, the camp seeks to orient freshmen to school life and to instill a sense of pride in A&M and its traditions. Freshmen who participate are bussed to Lakeview Assembly near Palestine for the 3-day orientation. In addition, the Corps of Cadets has conducted an orientation program called F.O.W., or Freshman Orientation Week, since 1977. It is an optional program held the week before classes begin to give new students an overview of A&M and help them start their college careers positively.

THE BATTALION

The student newspaper, the *Battalion*, began distribution on October 1, 1893. A prior paper, the *Texas Collegian*, had appeared in 1879. Ernest Bruce was the first editor of the *Battalion*, which was mainly a literary publication until 1904, when the Assocation of Former Students took over sponsorship and made it a weekly newspaper. It is now a student publication supervised by the Director of Student Publications, designed to provide staff members with opportunities to learn newspaper management and responsibility along with writing and editing.

THE RING

The original A&M Class Ring, featuring the intertwined AMC letters, was designed by the Class of 1889. In 1894, E. C. Jonas, a senior, designed the first Ring to feature the symbols now used. Unlike other college students, who may choose from many ring designs, all graduates at A&M wear rings of one design. The Ring serves as a common link for former students: when an Aggie sees a Ring on another Aggie, a spontaneous reunion occurs.

Each item on the Ring is a symbol. *The Texas Aggie* of October, 1969, described these symbols as follows:

The Shield on the top of the ring symbolizes protection of the good reputation of the Alma Mater. The 13 stripes in the shield refer to the 13 original states and symbolize the intense patriotism of graduates and undergraduates of A&M. The five stars in the shield refer to phases of development of the student; mind or intellect, body, spiritual attainment, emotional poise, and integrity of character. The eagle is symbolic of agility and power, and ability to reach great heights and ambitions.

One side of the ring symbolizes the seal of the State of Texas authorized by the constitution in 1845. The five-pointed star is encircled with a wreath of olive or laurel leaves symbolizing achievement and a desire for peace and liveoak leaves symbolizing the strength to fight. They are joined at the bottom by a circled ribbon to show the necessity of joining these two traits to accomplish one's ambitions to serve.

The other side with its ancient cannon, saber, and rifle symbolizes that the men of Texas fought for their land and are determined to defend their homeland. The saber stands for valor and confidence. The rifle and cannon are symbols of preparedness and defense. The crossed flags of the United States and Texas recognize the dual allegiance to nation and state.

The Senior Ring Dance is the annual highlight for seniors. It closes senior weekend, which begins with the Senior Bash, an event that raises money for the class, followed by the Senior Banquet. Until this time, seniors wear their rings with the inscription turned towards them. At the Ring dance, couples step into a huge replica of the Aggie ring; while standing there, the date removes the ring from the senior's finger and reverses it to reveal the seal and inscription to the world.

ELEPHANT WALK

The day before Bonfire, Aggie seniors congregate in front of the Academic Building. They form a single line and meander around the campus like dying elephants searching for a spot to spend their last days. This signifies that their usefulness to the Twelfth Man student body has ended and that they must make way for others. At times, juniors have taken a role in the senior Elephant Walk by following the elephants and ambushing them at every opportunity with shaving cream and water pistols. The elephants go through the fountain, down Military Walk to the Albritton Tower, and then to Kyle Field for Yell Practice. Still unwilling to end their Twelfth Man duties, the seniors then head to Duncan field and Bonfire for one more yell practice.

PART 4

SPORTS

SPORTS

The Aggie Spirit is most visible at sporting events. Win or lose, Aggies support their athletes. While best known for the prowess of their football and baseball teams, Aggies participate successfully in many college sports.

TWELFTH MAN

During sporting events, the student body is known as the Twelfth Man. The Twelfth Man supports every sport by displaying spirit. The following poem, which appeared in *The Corps at Aggieland* by Bill Leftwich and is entitled "The Twelfth Man," exemplifies this spirit. This poem, set to music, is sung when the Aggie team is outscored:

Texas Aggies down in Aggieland
We've got Aggie spirit to a man.
Stand united! That's the Aggie theme.
We're the 12th man on the team.
When we're down, the goin's rough and tough,
We just grin and yell we've got the stuff
To fight together for the Aggie dream.
We're the 12th man on that fightin' Aggie team.

The Twelfth Man tradition began during the final football game of the 1921 season, held on January 2, 1922. A&M was playing the Praying Colonels of Centre College in the Dixie Classic, a forerunner of the Cotton Bowl. As players were injured and reserves dwindled, Coach D. X. Bible called E. King Gill, a reserve sophomore fullback working in the press box as a spotter for a Waco sports writer, and asked him to suit up and be ready to play if needed. Under the stands, Gill switched clothes with injured Aggie captain Heinie Weir. Although he never played, legend has it that his loyalty and readiness spurred the Aggies to upset the undefeated and unscored-upon Praying Colonels by a 22-14 score.

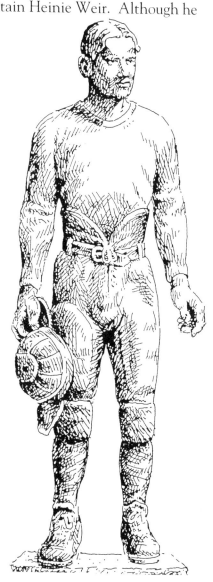

In 1941, Mrs. Ford Munnerlyn, the wife of an Aggie, wrote the words and music to the song "The Twelfth Man," which became one of the fight songs of the Corps. On March 1, 1980, the Twelfth Man Statue was dedicated as a gift from that year's Class. This likeness of E. King Gill stands at the north end of Kyle Field to remind Aggies of their constant duty to preserve the spirit of the Twelfth Man. That spirit continues today, as Aggie students stand during sports events to show their willingness to come to the aid of their athletic "comrades" when needed.

The Twelfth Man Kick-Off Team became part of the

football program in 1983 when Coach Jackie Sherrill wanted students to get more involved with the football team. Approximately 250 students try out for the Team each year. About 20-30 make the first cut, attend spring training, and return for the football season. They practice for 30 minutes before the regular team, then run drills with the players. At games they serve as the kick-off team. The Twelfth Man Team has started a new tradition: waving towels at football games.

D. X. BIBLE

One of A&M's first football coaches, D. X. Bible ranks among the most famous college coaches of all time. Bible began his career as the freshman coach at A&M in 1915. He went to Louisiana State University in 1916, but returned to A&M as head coach in 1917. Remaining through 1928 (he participated in World War I in 1918), Bible won every game in his first two seasons — those teams were unscored-upon — and five Southwest Conference Championships altogether. He left A&M for the University of Nebraska in 1929, and was head coach at t.u. from 1937 to 1946. He began the Twelfth Man tradition at A&M in the 1920's, and was one of the school's most beloved coaches.

FOOTBALL

The first recorded football game was held on November 29, 1894, against Ball High School of Galveston. A&M won 14-6. A&M also played its first game with t.u. in 1894, losing 38-0. The team had volunteer coaches until 1897, when C. W. Taylor was hired.

As A&M became a national competitor in football and other sports early in this century, its faculty became increasingly alarmed at the growing interest in sports. Like their counterparts today, they worried that students would misdirect their energies into athletic rather than academic pursuits. In response to this concern, a student-faculty committee was formed in 1902 to supervise athletic activities. In 1904, this group became the Athletic Council, which continues today to provide guidance for sports on campus.

Besides D. X. Bible, A&M has had many prominent coaches, including "Uncle Charlie" Moran (1909-14), Paul "Bear" Bryant (1954-57), Gene Stallings (1965-71), Emory Bellard (1972-78), and Jackie Sherrill (1982-88). The football team has won the Southwest Conference title 13 times and tied for it once. It won the National Championship in 1939, and it has been to the Cotton Bowl, including the original Dixie Classic, seven times.

KYLE FIELD

The site of home football games was chosen in 1904, when Edwin J. Kyle, chair of the Athletic Council, ordered a section of agricultural land fenced to provide a designated area for playing football. In 1906, the Bryan fair grandstands, providing seating for 500, were moved to Kyle Field. The second expansion, consisting of concrete stands on the west and east sides and the north end zone, was finished in 1929. The upper deck was built in 1954, and another enlargement in 1969 resulted in a seating capacity of 49,000. Astroturf was installed in 1970, and in 1979 the stadium was again enlarged to 72,000 seats with athletic facilities under the east stands. In 1983, the Spirit Flame was installed at the entrance to Kyle Field by that year's Class.

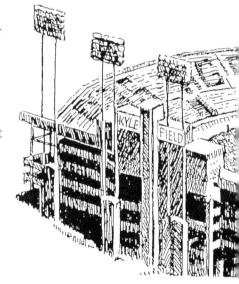

When the Aggie team scores, Aggies kiss their dates. This tradition is called "scoring." The old saying is "When the Aggies score on the field, the Aggies score in the stands, too." A legend is that during the years the team was not scoring much, Aggies got to kiss their dates after every first down.

YELL PRACTICE

Yell practice likely began before the turn of the century. An early tradition, it became a ritual after World War II. Yell practice is held immediately after supper on designated days to "fire up" the Corps and student body for football games. In the early days, freshmen who could still talk after a yell practice or game could expect consequences from upperclassmen.

Practices are led by men in white, known as Yell Leaders, who were first chosen in the 1920's. (Aggies do not have "cheer-leaders", or "cheers" which are called yells.) At that time only juniors and seniors could have dates at football games, so they decided to have the

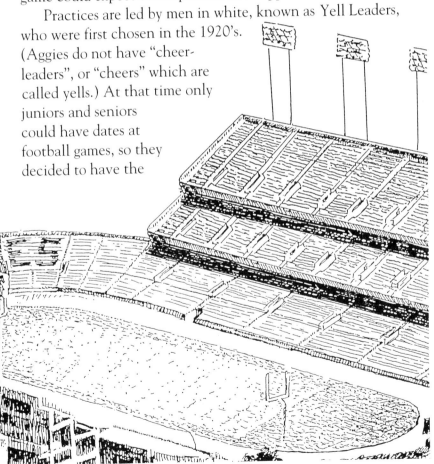

"fish" entertain the crowd at halftime. The "fish" became the first Yell Leaders. Now, five juniors and seniors are elected by the student body each year to serve as leaders. They lead the yells by using a hand signal which is passed through the crowd so everyone knows the right yell. The Yell Leaders also stop unsportsmanlike conduct by using a "rest signal," a single index finger held up.

Practices are held on the YMCA steps, in front of Goodwin and Sbisa Hall, at the Grove, and on Kyle Field. The band plays, the Yell Leaders lead practice, and pep talks are often given by prominent alumni. After a yell, each class displays its wildcatting method; this is a particular gesture adopted by that class — for example, shouting "aay" with hands clasped out in front like shooting a gun.

After winning a home game, Corps freshmen catch the Yell Leaders before leaving the field and carry them to Prexy's Triangle, with the Corps and band following to celebrate by throwing them in the fountain, known as the "Fish Pond." If the team is outscored, the Twelfth Man remains standing in the stadium for a short yell practice to show continuing support.

In the early years, to help the team in difficult situations, Yell Leaders and male students assumed a position called "squeeze Ags." If A&M lost, it was said to be because the participants didn't yell loud enough or squeeze hard enough. The "hump-it" position students now take involves bending over with hands on knees and keeping chins up and voices out.

MIDNIGHT YELL PRACTICE

The first Midnight Yell Practice was held in 1932. Before the t.u. game that year, a group of students gathered in the room of Peanut Owens, a junior yell leader, in Puryear Hall. They developed the idea of having the fish fall out and march around campus, ending with a yell practice in front of the YMCA at midnight. Though they said they couldn't officially sanction this activity, two senior yell leaders, Two Gun Herman and

Horsefly Berryhill, said they would be in the vicinity of the "Y" at midnight. At that time, the Corps were rousted from the dorms, the band showed up, and the tradition was begun.

Midnight Yell Practice is now held just before every home conference game. Band members with glowing torches and playing the Aggie War Hymn gather behind Duncan Dining Hall at 11:30 p.m.; students fall in behind, and the group marches to Kyle Field for yell practice. At some point during the practice, the lights are dimmed so that students can practice "scoring," the tradition of kissing one's date when points are scored on the playing field.

GIG 'EM, AGGIES

The spirit sign for Aggies is the "Gig 'Em" sign, a closed fist with the thumb pointing up.

YELLS

The first official college yell was formed in 1896. Its words were:

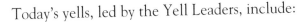

Rah! Rah! Rah!
Hi! Ho! Ha!
AMC
Boom! Cis! Ba!
College!

Today's yells, led by the Yell Leaders, include:

Gig 'Em
Yeaaaaaaaaaa, gig 'em Aggies!

Aggies
A-G-G-I-E-S
A-G-G-I-E-S
Yeaaaa, Fight 'em, Aggies!

Farmers Fight

Farmers Fight, Farmers Fight
Fight, Fight
Farmers, Farmers Fight!

Military

Squads left, squads right!
Farmers, farmers we're all right!
Load, ready, aim, fire, BOOM!
A & M, give us room!

Aggies don't "Boo" when they are upset with the action on the field. Instead, they give a "horse laugh" which goes:

Riffity riffity riff raff
Chiffity diffity chiff chaff
Riff raff
Chiff chaff
Let's give 'em a horselaugh.

This yell is followed by holding the hands over the head, as in prayer, and making a hissing sound.

BASEBALL

Baseball was played on campus several years before football. While possibly not the first game played, there was a known game on April 1, 1891 against Navasota. Baseball was thought to be on the decline when football was introduced on campus in 1893, but this proved not to be the case.

On March 21, 1978, the new baseball field opened. It was named for C. E. "Pat" Olsen (Class of '23), a former major league player who played with such greats as Babe Ruth and Lou Gehrig. The stadium seats approximately 5,000. Field lighting was added in 1980.

A&M has been the Southwest Conference Baseball champion seven times and tied three times. The baseball team is a national competitor at the highest levels.

T MEN

The T Association, organized on November 14, 1907, includes lettermen from all sports. Membership is open to current and former students who represented A&M in intercollegiate athletics. A "T" was awarded until 1915, when it was overlaid with the "AMC" to distinguish it from the "T" associated with t.u..

TEXAS AGGIE HEART AWARD

By vote of the varsity team, a senior football player is chosen each year to receive the "Aggie Heart Award," a special award based on the player's effort, desire, determination, and dedication to the team.

t.u. RIVALRY

The A&M/t.u. football rivalry began in 1894 when t.u. wanted a practice game before an interstate battle with Tulane. A&M brought a scrimmage squad of "Farmers" to Austin, losing 38-0. A&M beat t.u. for the first time in 1902, by a score of 11-0. The two teams have played annually since 1894, except for 1912-1914.

The A&M/t.u. game was held on Thanksgiving Day for the first time in 1919. This "Turkey Day" tradition continued until 1977, when the game was moved to Saturday for the first time, primarily to accommodate television.

In 1950, pranksters from A&M sowed the turf in t.u.'s Memorial Stadium in Austin with oats, which were quickly fertilized. Eventually, the oats grew out to spell "A&M," quite an embarassment to the t.u. team.

TEASIPS

"Teasip" refers to those who attend or have attended the University of Texas. The term originated in the late 1800's. Students attending t.u. were thought to lead an easy life compared to Aggies, who endured nine difficult months as freshmen and lived in tents. After World War I, the tents were replaced with shacks, known as "Hollywood Shacks." Aggies still refer to t.u. students and alumni as teasips or sips.

BEVO

The t.u. mascot got its name through the antics of A&M cadets in 1917. t.u. planned to brand a steer with the winning score of the 1916 game, which was 21-7. Three cadets located the steer a week before the 1917 game and branded it with A&M's 1915 winning score, 13-0. To use the steer as their mascot, t.u. students transformed the brand into BEVO, which at that time was the name of a near-beer. The brands were so unattractive that the t.u. Athletic Department slaughtered the steer and served a steak dinner at an A&M/t.u. get-together in 1921 designed to smooth relations between the two schools. The hide was shared, with A&M receiving the branded side and t.u. getting the head, which remains

mounted in the athletic offices. A steer named Bevo continues to serve as the t.u. mascot, and has been kidnapped a few times by A&M students before the Thanksgiving Day game.

BONFIRE

Bonfires to encourage support of sports events have been held since the early 1900's, when they were lit by excited students in anticipation of games. They became traditional in the 1920's, when the annual Bonfire before the t.u. game began. Bonfire was cancelled only once, in 1963.

In the early years Bonfire was built from trash scavenged by A&M students. A favorite item was an outhouse, and a Bonfire was once made by dismantling and burning a local farmer's barn.

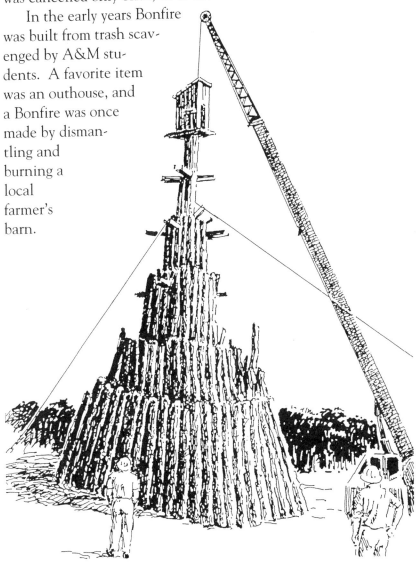

Following that stunt, Bonfire began to be built with logs cut specifically for that purpose. As the size of Bonfire grew, a center pole to support it was introduced in 1946. Cadets now prepare for Bonfire throughout the fall semester, gathering wood and setting up the site. The preparations become very intense in the last two weeks before Bonfire, including posting a nightly guard around the site to protect the logs from being set aflame by students from t.u. In 1933, Bonfire was ignited by t.u. students three weeks early, but it was quickly extinguished by Aggies. Now, Bonfire is made of approximately 9,000 logs that rise 55 feet. Five hundred gallons of diesel fuel and contaminated jet fuel are used to ignite the logs, and 500-1,000 people are involved in 24-hour shifts to build the structure and protect the site. These statistics prompted a listing in the *Guinness Book of World Records*.

Various groups of students form to make Bonfire a reality. Redpots — eight juniors and eight seniors — coordinate Bonfire, raise funds (90% comes from former students), choose the cutting site, gather the needed equipment, handle the press, ensure safety and watch construction activity. Brownpots are five seniors who manage the cutting sites. Yellowpots, consisting of a student from each residence hall, coordinate Bonfire for on-campus Aggies. Pinkpots are a junior and a senior who coordinate concessions and instruct women who want to help.

In the early years, Bonfire was held on the Simpson Drill Field in the evening, traditionally referred to as "dark-thirty." It is now held at the same time on the intramural field behind Duncan Dining Hall. According to *The Cadence*, a 1947-48 freshman handbook, "Bonfire symbolizes two things: a burning desire to beat the team from t.u., and an undying flame of love that every Aggie carries in his heart for his school." Legend has it that if Bonfire falls before midnight, t.u. will win the football game. This legend, however, has been proven untrue.

PART 5

THE CORPS

THE CORPS

The Corps of Cadets forms the nucleus of the Aggie Spirit and is the "bearer of the flame" of Aggie traditions. Its goal is to provide leaders for the state and the nation, and membership is based solely on individual worth and achievement. Until World War II, all undergraduates at A&M were required to join the Corps and were subject to the military regulations and discipline defined in the College "Blue Book." As enrollment became voluntary, the Corps became an even more elite and selective organization. Women were first admitted into the Corps in 1974.

Corps cadets participate in special activities designed to instill a spirit of loyalty and love for the school and the Corps. These spontaneous and comradely activities have evolved into many of the traditions now practiced at A&M.

FRESHMEN

Corps freshmen are called "fish." They are required to perform extra duties, including special drills and a strict program of behavior, designed to improve their military stance, to instill respect for military superiors, including the upperclassmen, and to teach them that to be a good leader, a person must first be a good follower. Some of the responsibilities of fish are as follows:

- Early every morning (approximately 6:25), one fish per unit must get up and blow the whistle for the first, second and third calls.

- On some days following morning call, they complete the "Campusology quiz" and, if a fish misses a question, he will receive corrective training.   If too many questions are missed, all fish receive such training.

- Freshman may give to upperclassmen only four answers: "Yes, sir"; "No, sir"; "No excuse, sir"; and "I hesitate to articulate for fear that I may deviate from the true course of rectitude.   In short, sir, I am a very dumb fish and do not know, sir."   The last answer is to be given as rapidly as possible.

- "Whipping out" is a ritual introduction required of each freshman who, upon meeting an upperclassman anywhere on campus, must offer his hand and shout, "Howdy, Fish so-and-so is my name, sir."

- On Fish Day, held on April 1, sophomores and freshmen swap places in the Corps hierarchy, and freshmen can boss sophomores.   Fish Day began in the 1930's when fish met in hand-to-hand combat with the sophomore class.   This activity was followed by a special Corps dinner.

- Fish carry Bonfire logs from the cutting area to the loading truck.

- At winning football games, fish gather at the edges of the field as the clock runs down; when it hits "0", they swarm onto the field, grab the Yell Leaders and carry them to the Fish Pond to throw them in.

SOPHOMORES

Sophomores are distinguished by their black braid and new

ability to give orders to fish while still having to take orders from juniors and seniors. Some of their duties are:

- to examine fish on mornings of formations.

- to protect the guidons.

- when fish make mistakes, to give the fish the correct training.

JUNIORS

Juniors have new-found freedom, as they don't have to answer to CQ — Call to Quarters for mandatory studying every night — as do Fish and Sophs. They are, however, threatened with the unauthorized activity of quadding, which involves being held below an upper story window from which fish from other outfits douse them with water. Their uniforms are highlighted by a white belt. Their duties include guarding the band during Midnight Yell Practice by locking arms and walking behind the band to keep others out.

SENIORS

Seniors are known as "Zips," "Top Dogs," and "Leather Legs." Their uniforms include the Aggie Ring and the impressive boots. Zips become "dead elephants" before Bonfire and wind through the campus in the Elephant Walk, they form "Bootline" at football games to welcome the team onto the playing field, and they stand in review during Final Review, the final pass-by as graduating seniors.

The Doherty Award, a cash award of $3,000, is presented to the outstanding senior cadet who is also receiving a commission in one of the armed services.

REVEILLE

In 1931, some cadets returning from Navasota in a Model-T could not stop when a stray puppy ran onto the road. They picked up the slightly injured dog and brought it to campus. The next morning at reveille, the puppy howled with the bugle call and was immediately christened Reveille. Reveille quickly befriended anyone in a cadet uniform and, only a few days after arriving at A&M, became the official mascot when he led the band onto the field at the t.u. game. Reveille's privileges on campus include admission to any building and choosing any bunk on which to nap. The unfortunate owner of that bunk cannot disturb Reveille, but must find another place to sleep, even if it is the floor.

Reveille wears a maroon and white blanket with "Texas Aggies" on both sides. Her care is the responsibility of Company E-2. The first Reveille died on January 18, 1944, after 13 years as mascot, and received a military funeral in the center of the

gridiron at Kyle Field. Reveille I is buried at the entrance to Kyle Field. Reveille II served from 1952-66, Reveille III from 1966-75, and Reveille IV retired in 1984 after nine years of service, passing away in 1989. All are buried at Kyle Field and honored with memorial stones there. The current Reveille V is a registered collie.

THE BAND

The largest military marching band in the nation, The Fightin'
Texas Aggie Band, a military unit within the Corps, was
formed in 1894 by Joseph Holick (Class of '98) and Arthur Jen-
kins. From its start as a 13-man group, it expanded in the
1930's to a 100-man unit, and now has grown to over 300.
The band offers no scholarships, has no auditions, and accepts
no music majors; its only requirements are previous marching
and playing experience. Housed as a military unit of the
Corps, it is a precision instrumentation and drill performance
band, and it is especially impressive because it exists at a school
with no music or fine arts program to generate members.

The Aggie Band lyre, which appeared in the late 1890's, is
worn by Band members. Since members come from all
branches of the services, the lyre distinguishes them. Band fish
receive their unshaved lyre after their first perfect halftime drill
and are allowed to wear the shaved lyre at Final Review the
second time around.

ROTC

ROTC was instituted at A&M in September, 1917. Participation in this military training program was mandatory for all
freshmen and sophomores. This did not affect membership in
the Corps of Cadets. In 1974, the Naval ROTC program was
established, allowing students to obtain a commission in any
branch of the service.

ROSS VOLUNTEERS

The oldest student organization in Texas was founded in 1887
as the Scott Guards, named after its founder, Colonel T. M.
Scott. In 1890, it was renamed the Ross Volunteers in honor of
the A&M President, Sul Ross. Membership is limited to outstanding junior and senior cadets who live by the motto "Sol-

dier, Statesman and Knightly Gentleman." The purpose of the Volunteers is to represent A&M in such functions as the Governor's honor guard, various parades around the state, and the "Firing Squad" during Silver Taps.

Members of the Ross Volunteers are identified by yellow and white cords on their uniforms. Because the Volunteers represent the live embodiment of dead heroes, freshmen and sophomore Corps members are not supposed to be able to "see" them when they are practicing or on show, as these lower-classmen have not yet made a commitment to the military.

SILVER TAPS

Silver Taps (pictured left) was first held in 1898 for Lawrence "Sul" Ross. This tribute is usually made to a deceased Aggie who is currently a student; rarely is it made to a former student. On the first Tuesday of each month, notices are placed at the base of the flagpole in front of the Academic Building. Campus flags are at half-mast. The ritual begins around 10:00 p.m. as students gather silently in front of the Academic Building, and friends and family of the deceased stand between the statue of Sul Ross and the front steps of the building. All lights in nearby buildings are turned out for the ceremony, and passing cars dim their lights.

As participants gather, music is played by the Albritton Carillon. The Firing Squad of the Ross Volunteer Company fires three volleys, and buglers play Taps three times from the dome of the Academic Building. Following Taps, the individuals leave the area silently.

The *Aggieland* of 1956 printed a poem, "Silver Taps," by Mabel C. Thomas:

Silently they gather, moving shadows
Under restless trees. Tight-lipped boys,
Full by day of rough, gay comradeship,
Have nothing to say tonight.

Clustered in hundreds round the Old Main Building,
They come to bid a last "Farewell"
To a fellow Aggie, whose footsteps
Will never tread familiar campus paths again.

Silently they wait, gazing far up at the dome
Rounded against the midnight sky.
The hour strikes, and four straight figures
Move to the corners of the turret,

Raising silver trumpets to their lips.
And then, tearing at the heart as does no other sound,
The notes come clear and sweet, and sad;
Silver Taps for one more Aggie who has gone

To join the bright battalion in the sky,
Where brave young men need never die.
Then, as the last, long unearthly note
Fades into the night, the cold dark silence bursts,
And guns send forth their final grim salute!
Stand at attention Aggies! Once more we honor them,
The Silver Taps Battalion of Texas A&M.

MUSTER

The Aggie Muster Ceremony is held around the world, wher-
ever Aggies gather each year, on April 21, San Jacinto Day,
the anniversary of the Texas victory of Sam Houston over
Santa Anna's army at San Jacinto. The ceremony honors
Texas heroes and deceased A&M students, and allows former
Aggies to relive their college days and renew their pledges of
loyalty and friendship to each other and to A&M.

Muster began in 1883 when Aggies met on June 26.
These meetings began as parties and banquets held during
commencement. In the late 1890's, the tradition was set for
the permanent date of April 21 to honor the freedom of Texas
and all Aggies who died the previous year. Muster has been
held in European foxholes in World War I, and during World
War II a ceremony was conducted on Corregidor Island in the
Philippines by 25 Aggies led by General George Moore (Class
of '08) in honor of Aggies who had fallen there. That Muster
inspired a world-wide Aggie Muster to be held each year.

Honored speakers for Muster have included General
Dwight D. Eisenhower, Chief of Staff of the U.S. Army, in
1946; Governor Allan Shivers in 1954; and Dr. E. King Gill
(Class of '14), the first Twelfth Man, in 1964. "Roll Call For

The Absent" honors the Aggies who have died during the previous year. A living comrade answers "Here" for the departed, signifying that the Aggie Spirit continues. On campus, the ceremony is held in the G. Rollie White Coliseum, where a candle is lit for each such student. The Ross Volunteer Firing Squad fires three volleys and the Silver Taps Bugle Team plays Taps.

MARCH TO THE BRAZOS

In 1931, some rowdy upperclassmen found some railroad torpedoes and rigged them to detonate around campus. After a few days of this, the brass called out Batteries A & B late at night to find the culprits. No one would confess, so in the rain and mud, the group was ordered to march until the guilty confessed. It marched all the way to the Brazos with no confession.

In subsequent years, cadets participated in a forced march to the Brazos River to keep them from playing April Fools' pranks on campus. After being discontinued for a few years, the March to the Brazos was reinstated on April 1, 1977, and is now held on the first Saturday in April. The cadets receive pledges of money for the march and donate them to charity.

MILITARY WALK

This street was used for many years by the Corps of Cadets when marching to meals at Sbisa Dining Hall. Markers were placed at each end of the walk by the Class of '36 to commemorate this tradition.

FINAL REVIEW

The last military review of the year, Final Review (pictured on page 70) occurs in May, following graduation. At this review, the entire Corps passes by and is promoted. Two reviews are held. In the first, cadets march in the position held during the school year; then, seniors line up in front of their outfits and sing "Auld Lang Syne," signifying that their participation in the Corps of Cadets is over. For the second review, cadets take their roles for the next year. Graduating seniors serve as reviewing officers for the new seniors, juniors, and sophomores as they pass in review. Juniors don boots and gold and black braid, sophomores wear white belts and braid, and fish get braid and Private brass. This is the only time that the Corps marches without a freshman class.

In the yearbook *Aggieland* of 1951, Steve C. Hoff described Final Review in this poem:

They are playing Alma Mater,
    You can hear the Aggie tune.
While they're standing at attention,
    'Neath the skies of Texas' June.

Now they're marching down the drill field,
    To the music of the band,
Past the Mothers and the Fathers
    Of the sons of Aggieland.

Past the spurred and booted seniors,
    Formed in an ordered line,
While their comrades do them honor,
    For the last and final time.

Four years of work are over,
    Four years of joy and pain,
And the spurred and booted seniors
    Ne'er will tread that field again.

Many a heart is filled with sadness,
    Many an eye is wet with dew,
As the Aggies dip their colors
    In the Seniors' last review!

COMMISSIONING

Commissioned seniors attend the Commissioning Ceremony after Graduation exercises. Not all Corps members go into the military. After the sophomore year, Corps members not planning a military career are allowed to remain in the Corps as "D&C," which means Drills and Ceremony.

Each senior being commissioned repeats the Oath of Office:

I, _____,
having been commissioned an officer
in the Armed Forces of the United States,
do solemnly swear (or affirm) that I will support and defend
the Constitution of the United States
against all enemies, foreign or domestic,
that I will bear true faith and allegiance to the same;
that I take this obligation freely,
without any mental reservation or purpose of evasion;
and that I will well and faithfully
discharge the duties of the office
upon which I am about to enter;
so help me God.

CORPS TRIPS

Members of the Corps attend out-of-town football games. The first Corps Trip was in 1887, when the student body descended on Dallas during the state fair. The trips are taken to show the support of the Twelfth Man. On game day, cadets conduct a parade, then yell for the team at the game.

The following poem is read at Bonfire and signifies the eternal comradeship of Aggies everywhere:

The Last Corps Trip

It was Judgment Day in Aggieland and tenseness filled the air;
All knew there was a trip at hand, but not a soul knew where.
Assembled on the drill field was the world-renowned
     Twelfth Man,
The entire fighting Aggie team and the famous Aggie band.
And out in front with Royal Guard the reviewing party stood;
Saint Peter and his angel staff were choosing bad from good.
First he surveyed the Aggie team and in terms of an angel swore,

"By Jove, I do believe I've seen this gallant group before.
I've seen them play since way back when, and they've always
     had the grit;
I've seen 'em lose and I've seen 'em win, but I've never seen
     'em quit.
No need for us to tarry here deciding upon their fates;
'Tis as plain as the halo on my head that they've opened
     Heaven's gates."
And when the Twelfth Man heard this, they let out a mighty yell
That echoed clear to Heaven and shook the gates of Hell.
"And what group is this upon the side," Saint Peter asked
     his aide,
"That swelled as if to burst with pride when we our judgment
     made?"
"Why, sir, they're the Texas Aggies who are known both far
     and wide
For backing up their fighting team whether they won or lost
     or tied."
"Well, then," said Saint Peter, "It's very plain to me
That within the realms of Heaven they should spend eternity.
And have the Texas Aggie band at once begin to play
For their fates we too must decide upon this crucial day."
And the drum major so hearing slowly raised his hand
And said, "Boys, let's play the Spirit for the last time in
     Aggieland."
And the band poured forth the anthem in notes both bright
     and clear
And ten thousand Aggie voices sang the song they hold so dear.
And when the band had finished, Saint Peter wiped his eyes
And said, "It's not so hard to see they're meant for Paradise."
And the colonel of the Cadet Corps said as he stiffly took
     his stand,
"It's just another Corps trip, boys. We'll all march in behind
     the band."

INDEX